Flavour Fix Your Burger

Also by Voula Halliday

Eat at Home: More than 150 recipes

Greek Spoon Sweets: A Recipe Card Collection

Flavour Fix Your Burger

make every bite the best

Voula Halliday

Cast Iron Press
Peterborough and the Kawartha Lakes, Ontario

CAST
IRON
PRESS

Library and Archives of Canada Cataloguing in Publishing data is available upon request.

ISBN 978-0-9878393-2-9 (paperback)

Made in Canada.

For bulk orders or inquiries, contact voula@eatathome.ca

Cover design: Ruth Dwight
Cover art (burger) and interior layout: Voula Halliday
Copy editor: Tracy Bordian/At Large Editorial Services
Proofreader: It Takes a Village

CAST
IRON   Published by Cast Iron Press
PRESS   www.eatathome.ca

For Maxine

CONTENTS

HOW TO USE THIS COOKBOOK

My quintessential meal delivers results without fuss, using accessible and (mostly) healthful ingredients. It is well-balanced and tasty, providing nourishment and joy with each bite, fulfilling hunger and my desire for all things crave-worthy, without costing a fortune. With that in mind, when the goal is to eat and the problem I am trying to solve is how to make something simple, nutritious, filling, and delicious, the solution is one of my favourite things: a burger.

Flavour Fix Your Burger is my definitive guide to making the absolute best-tasting burgers.

In this book, you'll find recipes, tips for making
and seasoning perfect patties to suit any palate,
and many mouth-watering ways to prepare
the best homemade burgers.

Start by exploring **Make Every Patty The Best**.
This section has something for everyone, including recipes for plant-based, salmon, chicken and turkey, beef, pork, or lamb patties. Once you've decided what kind of patties you'd like to make, you can choose how to flavour them using any one of the Flavour Fixes in the **Flavour Fix It** section. The choices are enticing and appetizing.

Flavour Fixes are easy-to-use seasonings, pastes, sauces, condiments, and spreads that will transform your burgers into something sensational with little effort.

I've developed each Flavour Fix recipe using thoughtfully chosen ingredients, without artificial additives or preservatives. These delicious flavour-forward recipes will boost your burgers from bland to remarkable.

Following Flavour Fix It, you'll find three more sections devoted to building even more flavour into your burgers:

- **Top It Up** and **Slather It with Sauce** detail all the delectable ways you can load up your burgers to make every bite the best, whether you make your own patties or buy them pre-made from your butcher or grocer.

- **Bundle Your Burger** provides many bun options and bun alternatives to complete your burger creations.

With the 25 recipes in this book, you can create over 100 unique burger combinations. Whether novice or expert cook, you'll find each Flavour Fix easy to prepare, easy to use, and wonderfully versatile.

I welcome you to contact me with questions or to share your comments and photos of your Flavour Fix burgers with me. I can't wait to see how you Flavour Fix your way to mealtime bliss.

Voula Halliday

Find me @voulahalliday
www.voulahallliday.com
www.eatathome.ca

Make Every Patty The Best

Patties, the main feature of any burger, can be made from ground meat (what we call a hamburger) or anything else you can layer between a bun. In this section, I provide recipes for making the best patties, including plant-based, fish, chicken or turkey, beef, pork, or lamb.

TIPS

There are three different varieties of paprika: sweet paprika is made from ground dried sweet peppers; smoked paprika is made with oak wood smoked peppers; and hot or Hungarian hot paprika is spicy and available sweet or smoked.

Both tamari and soy sauce are made from fermented soybeans. Tamari is usually gluten-free and has a richer flavour than soy sauce (which tends to be salty). Tamari is sometimes made with a small amount of wheat; if you have a sensitivity or allergy to wheat, check the label on the bottle before buying.

Black Bean and Quinoa Burgers

Delicious, hearty, satisfying—this burger is a favourite among vegans and vegetarians, and meat lovers enjoy it too. These patties can be made 100% gluten-free, as well as made ahead and frozen.

Makes enough for 4 burgers

2 Tbsp ground flaxseed
3 Tbsp water
19-oz can black beans, rinsed and drained
⅓ cup finely chopped yellow or red onion
2 cloves garlic, minced
2 Tbsp chickpea flour or unbleached all-purpose flour
2 Tbsp Flavour Fix of your choice
1 tsp smoked paprika (see Tip)
½ tsp sea salt
½ tsp finely ground black pepper
2 Tbsp barbeque sauce
1 Tbsp tamari or light soy sauce (see Tip)
1½ cups chilled cooked quinoa

In a small bowl, stir together ground flaxseed and water. Set aside for 5 minutes for the flax to absorb the water.

Place flaxseed mixture, beans, onion, and garlic into the bowl of a food processor fitted with the steel blade. Pulse just until beans are well chopped, not mushy. Transfer mixture to a large bowl.

Add flour, Flavour Fix, paprika, salt, pepper, barbeque sauce, and tamari. Stir until combined, and then stir in cooked quinoa.

To make sure your patty has all the flavour you desire, taste test your mix by following the instructions on page 8.

Divide mixture into 4 even portions and shape into patties about ½ inch thick. Cover and refrigerate for at least 2 hours or overnight.

Cook in a Pan
Lightly coat a 12-inch frying pan with oil and set over medium-high heat. Once pan is hot, carefully lay burgers down, cover pan with lid, and cook, without moving, for 4 to 6 minutes per side, until burgers are hot throughout and lightly browned.

Cook on the Grill
Oil your grill well and then preheat a barbeque to medium-high. Grill burgers with the lid down for 4 to 6 minutes per side, until heated through and lightly browned.

Taste Test It First!

A taste test is a great way to determine if you have added enough seasoning to your burger patty mixture.

Before dividing the mixture into 4 portions, remove about 1 Tbsp and press it into a ½-inch round. Set a small frying pan over medium heat, and once the pan is hot, add the patty mixture and cook briefly, no more than a minute per side, just until cooked through. Remove the pan from the heat. When the sample has cooled, taste to determine if you need to add more flavour.

If you plan to increase the amount of flavouring, I suggest adding 2 tsp and taste testing again. It's easier to add seasoning but impossible to remove if you overdo it.

Portobello Burgers

Nature has provided a juicy, flavourful, and fuss-free alternative to making your own patties. It is the portobello mushroom. These mushrooms require only a few simple steps to prepare, and they provide a perfect base for adding any Flavour Fix. Their dense texture and savoury taste make these mushrooms perfect for the smoky sizzle of a grill.

Makes enough for 4 burgers

8 large portobello mushrooms, stems removed (see Tip)
2 Tbsp extra virgin olive oil
2 Tbsp Flavour Fix of your choice

Using a clean cloth or kitchen paper, gently wipe each mushroom cap to remove any dirt. With a small spoon or a grapefruit spoon, gently scrape and remove the gills from each cap and discard (see Tip). Arrange mushroom caps in a single layer, gill-side down, on a baking sheet.

TIP

You don't have to remove the gills of the mushroom, but it's a step I don't skip. Dirt can hide in the gills, something we'd all rather not bite into. Also, when cooked, the gills have a bit of a spongy texture and become inky dark, and the juices from the mushroom gills will add a dark tinge to everything they touch, which I find unappealing, so I avoid it.

In a small bowl, whisk together olive oil and Flavour Fix. If you are using a paste and it seems too thick to spread onto the mushrooms, add a bit more olive oil, about 1 tsp at a time, until you reach the consistency that makes it easy to brush onto the mushrooms.

Brush mixture onto each mushroom cap, top and underside, and then set aside for 15 minutes to marinate.

Cook in a Pan
Lightly coat a 12-inch frying pan with oil and set over medium-high heat. Once pan is hot, place 3 to 4 mushrooms into pan. Cook, without moving, for 3 to 4 minutes per side, until mushrooms have softened and are lightly browned. Repeat with remaining mushroom caps.

Cook on the Grill
Oil your grill well, and then preheat barbeque to medium-high. Grill mushrooms, without moving, for 3 to 4 minutes per side, leaving the grill lid up, until mushrooms have softened and are lightly browned.

To serve, top each bun with 2 mushroom caps and your choice of toppings (page 52) or slathers (page 74).

Salmon Burgers

I'm a grilled salmon fan, but I can get a bit bored of it sometimes. Making a salmon burger is a nice change, and it's always fun coming up with new Flavour Fix combinations. Just thinking about the combo of a warm-off-the-grill brioche bun, hugging a Jamaican Jerk–seasoned (page 48) salmon patty with Sweet and Savoury Onion Maple Spread (page 69) and Zesty Herb Mayonnaise (page 80) has me drooling my way to the kitchen.

Makes enough for 4 burgers

1½ lb skinless salmon fillet, cut into 1-inch pieces (see Tip)
⅓ cup plain breadcrumbs
1 large egg, lightly beaten
2 Tbsp Flavour Fix of your choice
2 Tbsp finely chopped fresh parsley leaves
2 Tbsp mayonnaise
2 tsp fresh lemon juice

Place one-third of the salmon pieces into the bowl of a food processor fitted with the steel blade. Pulse a few times, just until salmon is coarsely chopped. Transfer chopped salmon to a large bowl. Repeat in two more batches with remaining salmon.

Add breadcrumbs, egg, Flavour Fix, parsley, mayonnaise, and lemon juice to bowl with salmon, and stir until combined.

To make sure your patty has all the flavour you desire, taste test your mix by following the instructions on page 8.

Divide mixture into 4 equal portions and shape into patties about ½ inch thick. Cover and refrigerate for at least 2 hours or overnight.

Cook in a Pan
Lightly coat a 12-inch frying pan with oil and set over medium-high heat. Once pan is hot, carefully lay burgers down and cook, without moving, for 3 to 4 minutes, until lightly browned on one side. Using a spatula, carefully turn burgers over and cook for an additional 3 to 4 minutes, until flesh is opaque and internal temperature reaches 70°C (158°F) when tested with a cooking thermometer.

Cook on the Grill
Oil your grill well, and then preheat barbeque to medium-high. Grill burgers, without moving, for 3 to 4 minutes. Using a spatula, carefully turn burgers over and cook for an additional 3 to 4 minutes, until flesh is opaque and internal temperature reaches 70°C (158°F) when tested with a cooking thermometer.

TIP

If you are concerned there might be bones in your salmon, run your fingers over the flesh side. If you find a bone, pull it out using your fingers or a kitchen tweezer. For large bones, you'll find that making a small cut with the tip of a knife next to the bone makes it easier to remove.

Chicken or Turkey Burgers

If you are looking for a tasty and lighter alternative to a burger made with red meat, chicken or turkey burgers are a perfect option. To guarantee moist and juicy patties, I mix in mayonnaise and am careful not to overcook them. The Dijon in this recipe provides a tangy layer of flavour to poultry.

I like to keep the garlic and onion optional, depending on what Flavour Fixes I use for my burger creation.

Makes enough for 4 burgers

1 lb lean ground chicken or turkey
¼ cup mayonnaise
1 Tbsp Dijon mustard
1 clove garlic, minced (optional)
⅓ cup finely sliced green onions (green and white parts) or chopped yellow onion (optional)
2 to 3 Tbsp Flavour Fix of your choice
¼ cup unseasoned panko breadcrumbs (see Tip)

Using your hands, break ground meat into small clusters and place on a baking sheet in a single layer. Loosely cover meat with plastic wrap or a clean kitchen towel, and place in the refrigerator for about 1 hour before mixing with other ingredients.

In a small bowl, stir together mayonnaise, Dijon, garlic, onion, and Flavour Fix. Set aside.

Once meat is chilled, remove baking sheet from fridge. Add meat to bowl with mayonnaise mixture and breadcrumbs. Using a spatula, gently stir until ingredients are evenly distributed (be careful not to overwork the meat or it will become compressed and tough when cooked).

To make sure your patty has all the flavour you desire, taste test your mix by following the instructions on page 8.

Divide mixture into 4 even portions and shape into patties about ¾ inch thick. Cover and refrigerate for at least 2 hours or overnight.

Panko crumbs are made with white bread and without the crust. They are flaky and light. Regular breadcrumbs are made with any bread, crust included, that is finely ground and often dense. When making burgers, you can use either panko or breadcrumbs in your patties to provide extra tenderness. Panko crumbs have an airy crispness that I prefer with salmon burgers, and regular breadcrumbs provide more structure in chicken and turkey burgers.

Cook in a Pan
Lightly coat a 12-inch frying pan with oil and set over medium-high heat. Once pan is hot, carefully lay burgers down and cook, without moving, for 1 to 2 minutes, until lightly browned on one side. Using a spatula, carefully turn burgers over and cook for another 1 to 2 minutes. Once burgers are lightly browned on both sides, reduce the heat to low and cover the pan with a tight-fitting lid. Cook, covered, for another 4 minutes (do not lift the lid).

To test for doneness, insert a cooking thermometer into side of burger; chicken or turkey burgers are done when thermometer reads 74°C (165°F). Transfer cooked burgers to a plate, cover loosely with foil, and rest for 3 to 5 minutes before serving.

Cook on the Grill
Oil your grill well, and then preheat the barbeque to medium-high. Carefully lay burgers onto grill, cover with the lid, and cook, turning once, for 4 to 6 minutes per side. To test for doneness, insert a cooking thermometer into side of burger; chicken or turkey burgers are done when thermometer reads 74°C (165°F). Transfer cooked burgers to a plate, cover loosely with foil, and rest for 3 to 5 minutes before serving.

How to Make The Best Meat Patties

There are many ways to season, prepare, and present a burger, and you'll find that no two burger creations will be the same. The process is delightfully uncomplicated, and the results are always gratifying, which makes cooking burgers at home worthwhile.

While every burger this book inspires you to make will be its own unique and delicious combination of flavours and textures, you can take some simple steps to ensure that your meat patties—the foundation of your burger—are fantastic every time. Here are my top tips:

1. The quality of the meat you use will define how good your burger patty tastes.
2. How the meat is prepared will affect how juicy and tender every bite will be.

This isn't to say that only expensive cuts of meat make the best patties—I assure you that a burger doesn't have to be costly to be succulent.

Store-bought pre-ground meat, available refrigerated or frozen, is a convenient option and will produce a decent burger, but the way it's processed and packaged, usually rather tightly, produces a denser patty. I explain how to handle this and any ground meat so you still get the best texture possible, even when it's not freshly ground.

There are two other options to consider, instead of purchasing pre-ground meat:

1. Ask your butcher for advice on the best cut to consider, one that provides a reasonable fat content. Once you've made your selection, ask the butcher to grind the cut of your choice to medium or coarse grind (this helps to maintain moisture during cooking).
2. Grind your meat at home using a food processor or a meat grinder. If you have the time, you can also finely chop meat by hand.

When it comes to choosing cuts of meat, the following are your best options for producing the tastiest burgers:

Beef: preferably chuck (shoulder cut)
Pork: shoulder or leg cut
Lamb: shoulder or leg cut

Generally, for making juicy, tender patties, about 20% fat is a good standard to go by. So look for a ratio of 80 to 85% lean meat to 15 to 20% fat.

Grinding Meat at Home Using a Food Processor

Cut meat into small pieces, about ½ inch, and then spread out in a single layer over a small, rimmed baking sheet (make sure pieces aren't piled on top of each other). Place in a freezer for about 20 minutes, until meat is firm but not completely hardened.

Remove meat from freezer, and then transfer a small amount into the bowl of a food processor fitted with the steel blade. Pulse a few times, stir the meat, and pulse again until the meat is coarsely chopped. Place chopped meat back onto baking sheet in a single layer (not piled up). Repeat the process in 2 to 3 more batches until all the meat is chopped.

Once all the meat is chopped, remove and discard any bits of gristle. If you aren't making your burger patties right away, cover and refrigerate meat until ready to use. Use within 2 days or store in an airtight container in the freezer for up to 4 months. When ready to prepare your burger, remove chopped meat from the refrigerator.

TIP

It's always best to work with chilled meat to keep the bits of fat from softening and incorporating into the meat before the cooking process begins—we want the fat to melt into the meat when the patty hits the grill, which helps to maintain moisture during cooking. Also, keeping the patty chilled until you are ready to cook will help to retain its shape.

Seasoning Your Burger Patties

Many burger purists will tell you they don't add seasoning to ground meat because they want to avoid overhandling and compressing the meat while combining ingredients. I say you can stir anything into ground meat to enhance the flavour as long as you don't over-mix or knead the mixture. It will be fine. (See my taste-testing Tip on page 8.)

Dry seasonings can be sprinkled over chopped meat while it is spread out on the baking sheet. This makes it easier to avoid handling the meat too much, and if you stir with a rubber spatula or a wooden spoon, rather than your hands, you won't warm the meat. When meat is cold, the fat throughout won't melt until heated. This helps maintain moisture during cooking.

Seasoning pastes require a bit more effort to blend in, but if you handle the mixture as lightly as possible, you won't end up with a tough burger. (See my Tip below.)

You will notice that my Flavour Fixes omit salt. Adding salt to the seasoning in the meat mixture can cause the meat to become springy because salt removes water and binds proteins together. Instead, I suggest you sprinkle salt (and pepper, if you wish) onto your burger patty after it is shaped and before it is cooked. This way, it will stay tender.

If your seasoning paste seems thick, combine it with 1 or 2 Tbsp mayonnaise (per 1 lb meat). This will make it easier to blend in the Flavour Fix without overworking the meat.

Shaping Your Burger Patties

Once your meat is flavoured, divide it into 4 equal portions, shape each one into a loosely packed round, and gently flatten.

Using your fingertips, make a slight indentation into the centre of each patty, pressing only two-thirds of the way down into the patty. This step will help keep the patty from shrinking into a ball when cooked.

Keep prepared patties refrigerated until ready to use. When meat is cold, the fat throughout won't melt until heated. This helps maintain moisture during the cooking. Also, keeping patties chilled until you are ready to cook will help to retain their shape.

Freezing Your Burger Patties

Cut parchment paper into 5 equal squares, making them large enough to cover the diameter of your patty. Layer the pieces of parchment in between each patty and stack them. Cover in plastic wrap, and then place in a freezer bag. When putting them into the freezer, ensure they are sitting flat and that nothing is squishing them so that they keep their shape. Thaw overnight in the refrigerator or cook from frozen.

When cooking burger patties from frozen, add 4 minutes to the overall cooking time.

Cooking Your Burger Patties to the Right Temperature

You can avoid upset tummies (and all that other not-nice stuff) by testing your meat for doneness using a digital food thermometer. Cook your burgers until they reach the following standard food-safe internal meat temperatures:

Chicken and turkey: 74°C (165°F)
Beef, pork, and lamb: 71°C (160°F)

Follow each recipe's cooking guidelines.

TIP

It's always best to work with chilled meat to keep the bits of fat from softening and incorporating into the meat before the cooking process begins—we want the fat to melt into the meat when the patty hits the grill, which helps to maintain moisture during cooking. Also, keeping the patty chilled until you are ready to cook will help to retain its shape.

Beef Burgers

Pre-made or hand-chopped, stuffed or smashed, all kinds of recipes claim to be the best burger recipe ever, but I maintain that the best is always a matter of personal taste, time, budget, and mood of the day. There are weeknights when a prepared frozen patty from my butcher is precisely what I want—convenient and satisfying—and then there are leisurely weekends when I have the time to prepare my own from scratch. This is the beauty of a simple classic beef burger: several good-quality options are available anytime.

Makes enough for 4 burgers

1 lb lean ground beef
2 to 3 Tbsp Flavour Fix of your choice

If you use pre-ground meat to make burgers, break meat into small clusters and place on a baking sheet in a single layer. Loosely cover meat with plastic wrap or a clean kitchen towel, and place in the refrigerator for about 1 hour to ensure it is well chilled.

If you are using meat you have ground or chopped yourself (see page 19), remove the baking sheet with the chopped meat from the refrigerator.

Sprinkle dry seasoning over chilled chopped meat while it is spread out on the baking sheet. Gently mix with a rubber spatula or a wooden spoon until evenly distributed.

If using a seasoning paste (see Tip page 20), add paste to a large bowl, place meat in small chunks on top, and stir gently using a rubber spatula or a wooden spoon until well combined.

To make sure your patty has all the flavour you desire, taste test your mix by following the instructions on page 8.

Divide into 4 equal portions, shape into loosely packed rounds, and then gently flatten.

Using your fingertips, make a slight indentation into the centre of each patty, but press only two-thirds of the way down. This step will help keep the patty from shrinking into a ball when cooked.

Keep prepared patties refrigerated until ready to use.

Cook in a Pan
Lightly coat a 12-inch frying pan with oil and set over medium-high heat. Once the pan is hot, carefully lay burgers down and cook, without moving, for 1 to 2 minutes, until lightly browned on one side. Using a spatula, carefully turn the burgers over and cook for another 1 to 2 minutes. Once the patties are lightly browned on both sides, reduce the heat to low and cover the pan with a tight-fitting lid. Cook, covered, for another 4 minutes (do not lift the lid). To test for doneness, insert a cooking thermometer into side of burger; beef burgers are done when thermometer reads 71°C (160°F). Transfer cooked burgers to a plate, cover loosely with foil, and rest for 3 to 5 minutes before serving.

Cook on the Grill
Oil your grill well, and then preheat barbeque to medium-high. Carefully lay burgers onto grill, cover with the lid, and cook, turning once, for 4 to 6 minutes per side. To test for doneness, insert a cooking thermometer into side of burger; beef burgers are done when thermometer reads 71°C (160°F). Transfer cooked burgers to a plate, cover loosely with foil, and rest for 3 to 5 minutes before serving.

Pork Burgers

If you are a fan of pork and are familiar with cooking it, you'll know that the fat marbled through the meat adds lots of flavour and juiciness. Some recipes that use ground beef will include a portion of ground pork mixed in to enrich the flavour. Of course, you can combine half beef and pork if you wish, or go "whole hog" to make a delicious pork burger, as I do in this recipe.

Makes enough for 4 burgers

1 lb lean ground pork
2 to 3 Tbsp Flavour Fix of your choice

If you use pre-ground meat to make patties, break meat into small clusters and place on a baking sheet in a single layer. Loosely cover meat with plastic wrap or a clean kitchen towel, and place in the refrigerator for about 1 hour to ensure it is well chilled.

If you are using meat you have ground or chopped yourself (see page 19), remove baking sheet with chopped meat from the refrigerator.

Sprinkle dry seasoning over chilled chopped meat while it is spread out on the baking sheet. Gently stir with a rubber spatula or a wooden spoon until evenly distributed.

If using a seasoning paste (see Tip page 20), add paste to a large bowl, place meat in small chunks on top, and stir gently using a rubber spatula or a wooden spoon until well combined.

To make sure your patty has all the flavour you desire, taste test your mix by following the instructions on page 8.

Divide into 4 equal portions, shape into loosely packed rounds, and then gently flatten.

Using your fingertips, make a slight indentation into the centre of each patty, but press only two-thirds of the way down. This step will help keep the patty from shrinking into a ball when cooked.

Keep prepared patties refrigerated until ready to use.

TIP

It's always best to work with chilled meat to keep the bits of fat from softening and incorporating into the meat before the cooking process begins—we want the fat to melt into the meat when the patty hits the grill, which helps to maintain moisture during cooking. Also, keeping the patty chilled until you are ready to cook will help to retain its shape.

Cook in a Pan
Lightly coat a 12-inch frying pan with oil and set over medium-high heat. Once the pan is hot, carefully lay burgers down and cook, without moving, for 1 to 2 minutes, until lightly browned on one side. Using a spatula, carefully turn burgers over and cook for another 1 to 2 minutes. Once lightly browned on both sides, reduce heat to low and cover pan with a tight-fitting lid. Cook, covered, for

another 4 minutes (do not lift the lid). To test for doneness, insert a cooking thermometer into side of burger; pork burgers are done when thermometer reads 71°C (160°F). Transfer cooked burgers to a plate, cover loosely with foil, and rest for 3 to 5 minutes before serving.

Cook on the Grill

Oil your grill well, and then preheat barbeque to medium-high. Carefully lay burgers onto grill, cover with the lid, and cook, turning once, for 4 to 6 minutes per side. To test for doneness, insert a cooking thermometer into side of burger; pork burgers are done when thermometer reads 71°C (160°F). Transfer cooked burgers to a plate, cover loosely with foil, and rest for 3 to 5 minutes before serving.

Lamb Burgers

Making a lamb burger can feel like a luxurious treat without a hefty price tag. Lamb has a rich, earthy, grassy flavour that welcomes bold or adventurous seasoning, but it also is perfect with just salt and pepper, hot off the grill.
I encourage you to try any of my Flavour Fixes in these patties. They all go great with lamb.

Makes enough for 4 burgers

1 lb lean ground lamb
2 to 3 Tbsp Flavour Fix of your choice

If you use pre-ground meat to make patties, break meat into small clusters and place on a baking sheet in a single layer. Loosely cover meat with plastic wrap or a clean kitchen towel, and place in the refrigerator for about 1 hour to ensure it is well chilled.

If you are using meat you have ground or chopped yourself (see page 19), remove baking sheet with chopped meat from the refrigerator.

Sprinkle dry seasoning over chilled chopped meat while it is spread out on the baking sheet. Gently stir with a rubber spatula or a wooden spoon until evenly distributed.

If using a seasoning paste (see Tip page 20), add paste to a large bowl, place meat in small chunks on top, and stir gently using a rubber spatula or a wooden spoon until well combined.

To make sure your patty has all the flavour you desire, taste test your mix by following the instructions on page 8.

Divide into 4 equal portions, shape into loosely packed rounds, and then gently flatten.

Using your fingertips, make a slight indentation into the centre of each patty, but press only two-thirds of the way down. This step will help keep the patty from shrinking into a ball when cooked.

Keep prepared patties refrigerated until ready to use.

It's always best to work with chilled meat to keep the bits of fat from softening and incorporating into the meat before the cooking process begins—we want the fat to melt into the meat when the patty hits the grill, which helps to maintain moisture during cooking. Also, keeping the patty chilled until you are ready to cook will help to retain its shape.

Cook in a Pan

Lightly coat a 12-inch frying pan with oil and set over medium-high heat. Once the pan is hot, carefully lay burgers down and cook, without moving, for 1 to 2 minutes, until lightly browned on one side. Using a spatula, carefully turn burgers over and cook for another 1 to 2 minutes. Once lightly browned on both sides, reduce heat to low and cover pan with a tight-fitting lid. Cook, covered, for another 4 minutes (do not lift the lid). To test for doneness, insert a cooking thermometer into side of burger; lamb burgers are done when thermometer reads 71°C (160°F). Transfer cooked burgers to a plate, cover loosely with foil, and rest for 3 to 5 minutes before serving.

Cook on the Grill

Oil your grill well, and then preheat barbeque to medium-high. Carefully lay burgers onto grill, cover with the lid, and cook, turning once, for 4 to 6 minutes per side. To test for doneness, insert a cooking thermometer into side of burger; lamb burgers are done when thermometer reads 71°C (160°F). Transfer cooked burgers to a plate, cover loosely with foil, and rest for 3 to 5 minutes before serving.

Flavour Fix It

When I appeared on CBC television's award-winning show *Steven and Chris* in 2015, I launched the Flavour Fix concept to national and syndicated audiences worldwide. Shortly after, I dedicated a section of my first cookbook, *Eat at Home,* to Flavour Fixes. What I affectionately call the "magic helpers in my kitchen" was a hit for everyone who tried them. These perfectly balanced flavour creations have long been my reliable, fuss-free way to boost my home cooking. The feedback was tremendous, and that book section was so well received that it inspired me to develop a range of Flavour Fixes—and I'm sharing some of my favourites here.

Flavour Fix Everything!

All the Flavour Fixes in this cookbook have been created to boost any meal or snack so go ahead and experiment with them.

Here are a few suggestions:

- Sprinkle seasoning onto whole chicken before roasting, and onto tofu or sliced halloumi before grilling.

- Rub dry seasoning or paste onto ribs or pork tenderloin before cooking, or onto vegetables for grilling.

- Mix seasoning or paste into ground meat to make tasty meatballs.

- Stir dry seasoning or paste into soups, stews, or sauces to add bright flavour.

There's no limit to how you can incorporate any of my Flavour Fixes into your cooking. I like a dollop of the Caramelized Onion and Blue Cheese Butter (page 54) on a sizzling hot steak, and will use the Fresh Cucumber Sauce (page 55) or Curry Yogurt Sauce (page 79) as a dressing for potato salad or a cabbage slaw, or slathered on salmon or trout before grilling.

Use Flavour Fixes to spark your culinary creativity!

Greek Seasoning

I constantly crave Greek food, so to satisfy my longing, I combine traditional flavours and keep a bit of Greece within reach, in my spice drawer. The smell of this reminds me of my mother's roasted chicken and potatoes, and the sesame-sprinkled bread rusks we snacked on after Sunday School.

You'll need to begin this recipe a day before to have time to dry the zested lemon peel completely (see Method), or you can use store-bought dried lemon peel (sometimes called "granules").

MAKES ABOUT ¾ CUP

¼ cup dried lemon peel (see Method)
3 Tbsp dried oregano leaves
3 Tbsp dried parsley flakes
1 Tbsp raw white sesame seeds
2 tsp granulated garlic or garlic powder
2 tsp onion powder
2 tsp finely ground black pepper

Combine all ingredients in a bowl. Transfer to an airtight container and store in a cool, dry place for up to 2 months.

METHOD

Two Ways to Dry Citrus Zest

Overnight: Sprinkle finely grated zest onto a large plate and let sit out overnight or until it's dried. You will find stirring it after a few hours will help. Once completely dried, it's ready to be added to your Flavour Fix.

Quick method: Spread finely grated zest over a parchment-lined baking sheet. Place baking sheet on the middle rack of a pre-heated 250°F (130°C) oven and heat until the zest is dry. This will happen quickly, so start checking after 5 minutes and, if needed, every few minutes after. Once dry, remove baking sheet from oven and cool completely before combining with other ingredients.

Heavenly Herb Seasoning

Dried herbs can add lots of flavour to your food but only if fresh. Don't be tempted to make this seasoning with herbs you had long forgotten were in your pantry. Test your herbs before using them to make sure they are fresh and flavourful (see Tip) because this is a beautiful blend that can be used for more than just burgers. Add to salad dressings and sauces, or stir into softened butter for an herby spread.

MAKES ABOUT ¾ CUP

2 Tbsp dried oregano leaves
2 Tbsp dried parsley leaves
2 Tbsp dried thyme leaves
1 Tbsp dried dill weed
2 tsp dried basil leaves
2 tsp dried marjoram leaves
2 tsp dried rosemary leaves

Combine all ingredients in a bowl. Transfer to an airtight container and store in a cool, dry place for up to 2 months

 TIP

Dried herbs lose their flavour over time. Smelling your herbs is a good way to determine if they are still fresh enough to use. If you can't distinguish what the herb is by smell, then it's probably past its time.

Louisiana Seasoning

I cherish my copy of Paul Prudhomme's cookbook *Louisiana Kitchen.* When I first got the book, I used it often to cook up a feast for family and friends. The recipes became familiar, as did the delicious taste of Creole and Cajun cuisine. I created this blend to satisfy my appetite for the flavours I like so much.

MAKES ABOUT ¾ CUP

3 Tbsp sweet paprika
2 Tbsp dried thyme leaves
2 Tbsp granulated garlic or garlic powder
2 Tbsp onion powder
2 ½ tsp finely ground black pepper
2 ½ tsp ground cumin
2 ½ tsp dried sage leaves
1 tsp mustard powder

Combine all ingredients in a bowl. Transfer to an airtight container and store in a cool, dry place for up to 6 months.

VARIATION

To add spicy heat to this blend, stir in ¼ to ½ tsp cayenne pepper.

Moroccan Seasoning

I didn't realize this recipe would have such broad appeal when I included it in my first cookbook, *Eat at Home*. I've had so many people tell me they've used it in stews, soups, rice dishes, and even deviled eggs. My family loves it in lamb burgers or sprinkled on carrots or sliced sweet potato and onions before roasting.

MAKES ABOUT ¾ CUP

¼ cup dried parsley flakes
2 Tbsp granulated garlic or garlic powder
2 Tbsp ground coriander
2 Tbsp ground cumin
2 Tbsp sweet paprika
2 tsp finely ground black pepper
1 tsp ground allspice
1 tsp ground cinnamon (see Tip)
1 tsp sea salt

Combine all ingredients in a bowl. Transfer to an airtight container and store in a cool, dry place for up to 6 months.

TIP

We tend to associate cinnamon with baking, but this spice, which is the bark of an evergreen tree, also adds a fragrant and warm flavour to savoury dishes. It's a spice you'll find used throughout Moroccan cuisine.
Bonus: Cinnamon is loaded with antioxidants and other health benefits.

Shawarma Seasoning

Shawarma is a Middle Eastern dish of richly seasoned meat stacked in a cone shape, cooked on a vertical rotisserie, sliced, and then stuffed into a warm fresh pita. It is delicious, filling, and healthy. I couldn't resist mixing a batch of this delightful blend of herbs and spices to flavour my burger patties. Sometimes, I serve these in pita bread rather than tucking my patty into a bun.

MAKES ABOUT ¾ CUP

¼ cup dried parsley flakes
2 Tbsp ground coriander
2 Tbsp ground cumin
2 Tbsp smoked paprika or regular (sweet) paprika
1 Tbsp granulated garlic or garlic powder
2 tsp finely ground black pepper
2 tsp ground turmeric
2 tsp ground sumac (see Tip)
¼ tsp cayenne pepper (optional)
¼ tsp ground cinnamon

Combine all ingredients in a bowl. Transfer to an airtight container and store in a cool, dry place for up to 6 months.

TIP

Sumac is deep red in colour and tangy like lemon, with a pleasantly floral and earthy flavour that is quite appealing. Ground sumac, or sumac powder, is made from the dried berries of the shrub by the same name.

Smoked Paprika Seasoning

Smoked paprika doesn't provide the same char-grilled feeling we associate with summertime barbecues. Still, it makes up for the lack of a sizzling grill on days when the weather isn't conducive to outdoor cooking or when you want a shortcut to a smoky taste of a seasoned grill.

MAKES ABOUT ¾ CUP

3 Tbsp dried oregano leaves
3 Tbsp dried parsley flakes
2 Tbsp smoked paprika (see Tip)
2 Tbsp chili powder
1 Tbsp granulated garlic or garlic powder
1 Tbsp ground coriander
1 Tbsp ground cumin

Combine all ingredients in a bowl. Transfer to an airtight container and store in a cool, dry place for up to 6 months.

TIP

There are three different varieties of paprika: sweet paprika is made from ground dried sweet peppers; smoked paprika is made with oak wood–smoked peppers; and hot or Hungarian hot paprika is spicy and is available sweet or smoked.

Hot and Smoky Harissa Paste

Just a short distance from where we used to live in Sydney, Australia, is a restaurant called Radio Cairo, where I first tasted this versatile North African spice paste. While smoked paprika is not a traditional element of this paste, I like the smoky accent it adds. You can use this hot and garlicky condiment on just about anything.

MAKES ABOUT 1 CUP

1 large red bell pepper, cored, seeded, and roughly chopped
¼ cup extra virgin olive oil
¼ cup tomato paste
2 cloves garlic, coarsely chopped
1 Tbsp caraway seeds
1 Tbsp ground coriander
1 Tbsp ground cumin
2 tsp dried chili flakes
2 tsp smoked paprika

Place all ingredients in the bowl of a food processor fitted with the steel blade. Pulse until the mixture becomes a thick paste, scraping down the sides of the bowl as needed.

Transfer to an airtight container and store in the refrigerator for up to 2 weeks.

 VARIATION

To make a quick and tasty spicy mayonnaise, stir 1 tbsp of this paste into 1 cup of mayonnaise.

Indian Spice Paste

I love Indian food, and over the years I've learned how to prepare delicious meals from a myriad of cookbooks and the coveted knowledge shared with me by my friends. A savoury and well-balanced spice paste like this isn't difficult to prepare. I make this often to add to burger patties, but I'll also use it to season chicken wings or stir it into stews and soups.

MAKES ABOUT ½ CUP

3 cloves garlic, coarsely chopped
2 Tbsp coarsely chopped peeled fresh ginger
2 Tbsp tomato paste
2 Tbsp water
2 tsp garam masala (see Tip)
2 tsp ground coriander
2 tsp ground cumin
2 tsp ground turmeric
1 tsp dried chili flakes
1 tsp ground cinnamon

Place all ingredients in the bowl of a food processor fitted with the steel blade. Pulse until the mixture becomes a smooth, thick paste, scraping down the sides of the bowl as needed.

Transfer to an airtight container and store in the refrigerator for up to 2 weeks.

TIP

Garam masala is an aromatic blend of warming spices used throughout India to add flavour to curries or soups. There are many variations of this blend, and some are hotter than others. Curry, another traditional combination of dried spices used in India, contains turmeric, which adds a golden yellow hue to dishes. The main difference is that garam masala does not include turmeric.

TIP

Scotch bonnet peppers are extremely hot. If you aren't sure how much heat you can handle, start with just half the amount of hot pepper. If you prefer milder heat, substitute 1 jalapeño pepper. Also, keep in mind that the most potent heat in any hot pepper comes from capsaicin found in the seeds and the pith. To tone down the heat, remove these parts before using hot peppers, and consider wearing kitchen gloves when preparing them. Capsaicin can linger on your skin and cause a burning sensation.

Jamaican Jerk Paste

After trying different store-bought versions of Jamaican Jerk seasonings and discovering how much I loved the combination of warming spices and hot peppers, I began making my own with peppers from my garden. I tested varying amounts of heat and seasonings to create this flavourful, nicely balanced spiced paste.

MAKES ABOUT ½ CUP

8 green onions (white and green parts), coarsely chopped
1 Scotch bonnet pepper (see Tip)
¼ cup white vinegar
2 tsp ground allspice
2 tsp ground cinnamon
2 tsp granulated garlic or garlic powder
2 tsp ground nutmeg
2 tsp dried thyme leaves
2 tsp finely ground black pepper

Place all ingredients in the bowl of a food processor fitted with the steel blade. Pulse until the mixture becomes a smooth, thick paste, scraping down the sides of the bowl as needed.

Transfer to an airtight container and store in the refrigerator for up to 2 weeks.

Mustard and Herb Paste

The inspiration for this recipe comes from my husband, who often combines Dijon with fresh or dried herbs and smears it on meat before grilling. Dijon has a bit of a bite that works well with honey and herbs. If you aren't a fan of sweetness, you can skip the honey in this recipe. It will be just as delicious.

MAKES ABOUT ¾ CUP

2 cloves garlic, minced
½ cup Dijon mustard (see Tip)
¼ cup finely chopped fresh chives
¼ cup finely chopped fresh flat-leaf parsley leaves
2 Tbsp finely chopped fresh basil leaves
1 Tbsp brown mustard seeds (optional)
2 tsp finely chopped fresh rosemary leaves
1 tsp dried thyme leaves
2 Tbsp extra virgin olive oil
1 Tbsp liquid honey or pure maple syrup (optional)

Place all ingredients in a bowl. Using a fork, stir until the mixture is well combined.

Transfer to an airtight container and store in the refrigerator for up to 2 weeks.

Dijon mustard gets its name from the city where it originated in Burgundy, France. It is made with white wine and brown mustard seeds, and has a spicy and sharp flavour. Yellow mustard is made from white mustard seeds and vinegar. Turmeric is added for colour. They are quite different in flavour, so you can't easily rely on one as a substitute for the other.

Top It Up

Load your burger with delicious Flavour Fix toppings.
Use one, or more, to make every bite the best.

Caramelized Onion and Blue Cheese Butter	54
Fresh Cucumber Sauce	55
Honey Hot Chili Tomato Sauce	57
Marinated Cherry Tomatoes	59
Miso Magic Mushroom Sauce	61
Piperade	63
Spicy Pimento Cheese	65
Spinach, Dill, and Feta Spread	68
Sweet and Savoury Onion Maple Spread	69
Triple X Spicy Sambal	72

TIP

Blue cheese has a distinct sharp and salty flavour marbled into milky creaminess. To produce this cheese, a mould culture is added to cow, goat, or sheep's milk cheese and then left to develop and mature for several months. There are many blue cheeses, some more creamy than others and some less salty.

Caramelized Onion and Blue Cheese Butter

Most varieties of blue cheese can have a strong flavour, but when matched with the sweetness from caramelized onions and the richness of butter, the bite in this cheese mellows out. These ingredients combined become a subtle, well-balanced, and delicious spread.

MAKES ABOUT ¾ CUP

1 Tbsp extra virgin olive oil
1 small yellow onion, cut in half lengthwise and thinly sliced into strips
1 tsp finely chopped fresh thyme leaves
½ cup unsalted butter, at room temperature
¼ cup crumbled blue cheese (see Tip)
¼ tsp coarsely ground black pepper

Place oil and onion in a medium frying pan and set over low heat. Cook, stirring occasionally, until onion is soft, 15 to 20 minutes. Add thyme and cook for 5 more minutes, until onion starts to brown, stirring often to avoid burning. Remove from heat and set aside to cool to room temperature.

Transfer cooled onion mixture to the bowl of a food processor fitted with the steel blade. Add remaining ingredients. Pulse until smooth and well combined, scraping down the sides of the bowl as needed.

Transfer to an airtight container and store in the refrigerator for up to 2 weeks.

Fresh Cucumber Sauce

Light, refreshing, and "cool as a cuke," this sauce is best slathered straight from the fridge to enjoy the chilled sensation of cucumber, yogurt, lime, and mint. It's not just great for your burgers; this goes well with pork kebabs, grilled chicken, or lamb chops.

MAKES ABOUT 1 CUP

½ English cucumber or 3 small Lebanese cucumbers
½ cup plain Greek yogurt (see Tip)
¼ cup fresh lime juice
½ tsp sea salt
½ tsp finely ground black pepper
½ tsp ground cumin
½ tsp dried chili flakes (optional)
¼ cup finely sliced fresh cilantro leaves
¼ cup finely sliced fresh mint leaves

Peel and then cut the cucumber in half lengthwise. Using a small spoon, scoop out and discard the seeds. Coarsely chop the cucumber and place it in the bowl of a food processor fitted with the steel blade. Add yogurt, lime juice, salt, pepper, cumin, and chili flakes (if using), and process until creamy. Then add the cilantro and mint, and pulse a few times until combined.

Transfer to an airtight container and store in the refrigerator for up to 5 days. Serve cold or at room temperature.

Greek yogurt has a thick and creamy texture, sometimes almost as thick as whipped cream cheese. This is achieved when traditional yogurt, which isn't thick, is strained through a food-grade filter or fine cloth such as cheesecloth. Straining removes whey protein and lactose. What's left is a thick, tangy concentrated product with higher protein and less sugar than regular yogurt.

The milk fat percentage in Greek yogurt varies from 0% to 7 or 9%. What you use is entirely a matter of your taste and personal health preferences.

We so often hear that fat adds flavour, but if you ask me, tangy Greek yogurt, no matter how much fat it contains, is always tasty. When buying yogurt, look at the ingredients and avoid varieties that add fillers or thickeners, such as corn starch.

Bonus Tip:
Adding Greek yogurt is a healthy way to thicken hot soups and sauces, but the high protein content will cause it to curdle in high heat. Before mixing yogurt into your soup or sauce, ensure the mixture is warm, not hot. Bring yogurt to room temperature, and then stir a small amount of the warm soup or sauce into the yogurt. Once it's well combined, add the mixture to the soup or sauce and stir. Reheat over low heat, stirring often.

Honey Hot Chili Tomato Sauce

Sweetened with honey and made with a small but mighty combination of ingredients, this sauce delivers a spicy, savoury, sweet mouthful of flavour in every dollop. It's one of my favourite sauces.

This recipe makes a big batch, enough for sharing with family and friends. It's enough for 3 x 250 mL jars of sauce. Reduce the ingredients by half to make a smaller batch.

MAKES ABOUT 3 CUPS

1 kg ripe tomatoes (about 8 medium), coarsely chopped
8 cloves garlic, coarsely chopped
6 small red Thai chili peppers, coarsely chopped (see Tip)
1 cup liquid honey
2 Tbsp tamari (use reduced-sodium tamari, if you wish)
½ cup red wine vinegar or apple cider vinegar

Place tomatoes, garlic, and peppers into the bowl of a food processor fitted with the steel blade. Pulse until mixture becomes smooth. Pour into a medium heavy-bottomed saucepan, and set over medium-high heat.

Stir honey, tamari, and vinegar into tomato mixture. Bring to a boil, stirring occasionally, and then reduce the heat and simmer, uncovered for 40 to 60 minutes, stirring often, until mixture has thickened. (It will thicken a bit more after cooling, so consider how thick you'd like yours, and remove it from the heat just before it reaches the thickness you desire.)

Set aside to cool to room temperature, and then store in resealable jars in the refrigerator for up to 2 months.

You can reduce the heat in this sauce by using 3 or 4 Thai chili peppers instead of 6.

Marinated Cherry Tomatoes

Made with ingredients you probably have handy, marinated tomatoes are a fresh and tasty way to brighten your burgers. This makes a nice topping for avocado toast and is a great Flavour Fix to add when making a quick and delicious pasta salad.

MAKES ABOUT 1 CUP

1 cup cherry or grape tomatoes, sliced in half (see Tip)
¼ cup finely sliced fresh chives (optional)
1 small clove garlic, minced
2 Tbsp extra virgin olive oil
1 Tbsp balsamic vinegar
¼ tsp sea salt
¼ tsp finely ground black pepper

Add all ingredients to an airtight container. Stir to combine. Cover and refrigerate for at least 1 hour but not more than overnight.

TIP

Sometimes I roast my tomatoes whole before mixing up a batch of this salsa. The tomatoes burst a bit, and roasting brings out the sweetness in them. Heat oven to 375°F (190°C). Place tomatoes in a roasting pan. Drizzle with oil and roast just until tomatoes blister, about 15 minutes. Remove from the oven and set aside to cool before combining with the rest of your ingredients.

Miso Magic Mushroom Sauce

If you have my first cookbook, *Eat at Home,* you will have come across one of my favourite recipes: Sirloin with Mushroom Miso Sauce. I keep returning to the sauce from this recipe because I think it's incredible and versatile. The combination of miso and mushrooms is rich and flavourful. This sauce goes great with meat, chicken, fish, grilled tofu, or stirred into noodles.

MAKES 2 CUPS

1 cup vegetable or chicken broth (see Tip)
1 can (14 oz) coconut milk
3 Tbsp white miso paste (see Tip)
1 tsp dried thyme leaves
1 Tbsp extra virgin olive oil
2½ cups sliced fresh mushrooms (cremini or button, or a mix)
2 cloves garlic, minced
1 small yellow onion, finely chopped

Whisk broth, coconut milk, miso, and thyme in a bowl. Set aside.

Add oil to a large frying pan and set over medium-high heat. Add mushrooms, garlic, and onion. Cook, stirring occasionally, until mushrooms are browned, 5 to 6 minutes. Add broth mixture, bring to a boil, and then reduce the heat and simmer for 8 to 10 minutes, until sauce is thick. Remove pan from the heat and set aside to cool.

Transfer cooled sauce to an airtight container and store in the refrigerator for up to 2 weeks. Serve warm (reheat on low to ensure sauce does not separate).

Store-bought broths are usually high in sodium, so I haven't included additional salt in this recipe. Taste this sauce before serving to determine if you need to stir in some salt.

Miso is a fermented paste used throughout Asian cuisine. There are many types of miso, typically made with rice, barley, or soy. Shiro miso, also known as white miso, is the most common; it is milder in taste than another commonly found miso, Aka or red miso.

Piperade

Piperade originates from the Basque region of France and is a beautiful combination of Mediterranean sun-loving ingredients. A savoury topping, it's traditionally served with eggs or ham, but we use it on our burgers and almost anything else we can think of—it's that good.

MAKES ABOUT 5 CUPS

2 Tbsp extra virgin olive oil
2 yellow onions, cut in half lengthwise and thinly sliced into strips
1 large red bell pepper, cored, seeded, and cut into strips
1 large green bell pepper, cored, seeded, and cut into strips
2 cloves garlic, minced
2 Tbsp finely chopped fresh parsley leaves
1 tsp dried thyme leaves
1 can (28 oz) plum tomatoes, drained and coarsely chopped (see Tip)

Set a large frying pan over medium-high heat. Add oil and onions, and cook, stirring occasionally, until onions are translucent, about 8 minutes.

Stir in peppers, garlic, parsley, and thyme. Add tomatoes. Cover and cook, stirring occasionally, until peppers soften, about 8 minutes. Remove from heat and set aside to cool.

Transfer cooled piperade to an airtight container and store in the refrigerator for 3 days. This can be served cold or at room temperature, or you can reheat on low.

Store the tomato juice in an airtight container in the freezer and use it like a vegetable broth. I add it to soups, sauces, and stews.

Spicy Pimento Cheese

My friend Marcel is an exceptional cook. Everything he makes becomes something we wish to eat repeatedly. He introduced me to homemade spicy pimento cheese and inspired me to make this recipe. Top your burger with a generous dollop. I also strongly suggest you always keep some of this in the fridge for when you want a savoury snack on a cracker or a delicious grilled cheese sandwich.

MAKES ABOUT 3 CUPS

1½ cups extra sharp cheddar cheese, shredded
1½ cups Monterey Jack cheese, shredded
1 Tbsp dried chili flakes
2 tsp garlic powder
1 cup finely diced pimentos or roasted red peppers, drained (see Tip)
¼ cup mayonnaise
¼ cup finely sliced green onion (green and white parts)
1 Tbps finely chopped jalapeño pepper, seeds removed (for a milder heat)
2 tsp white wine vinegar
1 tsp fresh lemon juice
1 tsp Tabasco sauce
½ tsp Worcestershire sauce

Gently combine cheddar and Monterey Jack in a large bowl. Sprinkle with chili flakes and garlic powder, and then gently stir to evenly coat. Set aside.

Add pimentos, mayonnaise, green onion, jalapeño, vinegar, lemon juice, Tabasco, and Worcestershire to a medium bowl. Stir well, and then add to the cheese mixture. Gently stir until all ingredients are incorporated. Cover and refrigerate for at least 1 hour before serving.

Pimento will keep in an airtight container in the refrigerator for up to 2 weeks.

Pimentos, or pimientos as they are known in Portuguese and Spanish, are small, sweet, and delicious cherry peppers. They come roasted and peeled, available in jars. You can find them in the deli section of your grocery store or the same aisle as pickles, olives, and other condiments.

TIP

Romaine lettuce is tasty and packed with nutrients, and it's sturdy enough that you can sauté it, grill it, or chop it up and stir it into soup. I love it and use it any way I can. The Greeks make a salad called *Maroulosalata* (romaine salad), which has the same delicious flavours as this spread. This recipe is a hit made with either spinach or romaine lettuce.

Spinach, Dill, and Feta Spread

The first time I made this, I couldn't believe how delicious and satisfying it was. It is a beautiful flavour booster as a condiment, but you can also use it to make a grilled cheese sandwich or spread it on a toasted bagel for instant satisfaction. Think of it as the creamiest version of a filling in Greek spanakopita.

MAKES ABOUT 2 CUPS

1 cup crumbled feta cheese
1 cup plain Greek yogurt (see page 56)
1 cup packed finely chopped baby spinach or Romaine lettuce (see Tip)
2 green onions, finely sliced (green and white parts)
2 Tbsp finely chopped fresh dill (fronds and stems)
½ tsp finely ground black pepper
½ tsp sea salt

Add all ingredients to a bowl and stir until well combined. Transfer to an airtight container and store in the refrigerator for up to 2 weeks.

Sweet and Savoury Onion Maple Spread

Onions become mellow and sweet with slow cooking, and this is exactly how my daughter likes them, so I created this spread with her in mind. Fresh thyme and cider vinegar make this extra tasty. This is a versatile, easy-to-make onion condiment you can use on sandwiches, or to complement cheese or charcuterie.

MAKES ABOUT 1 CUP

2 Tbsp extra virgin olive oil
2 large yellow onions, cut in half lengthwise and thinly sliced into strips
2 cloves garlic, minced
2 Tbsp pure maple syrup (see Tip)
3 tsp finely chopped fresh thyme leaves
2 tsp apple cider vinegar
¼ tsp sea salt

Place oil, onions, and garlic in a medium saucepan over low heat. Cook, stirring occasionally, until onions are soft, about 25 minutes. Stir in maple syrup. Continue to cook, stirring occasionally, until very soft, about 15 minutes. Add thyme and cook for 5 more minutes, until onions start to brown, stirring often to avoid burning them. Stir in vinegar and salt. Remove from heat and set aside to cool to room temperature.

Transfer cooled mixture to an airtight container and store in the refrigerator for up to 2 weeks.

When the sap of the maple tree is boiled down, it becomes a naturally sweet and tasty syrup. Do not confuse this with commercially produced sugar syrups made with the addition of maple flavouring. Pure maple syrup is graded according to colour and flavour. Grade A maple syrup is generally extra light to medium in colour. Grade B is usually amber in colour. The deeper the colour, the slightly stronger the maple flavour. It doesn't matter what grade you use in the recipes in this book as long as you stick to using pure maple syrup.

If you aren't sure how much heat you can handle, reduce the amount of pepper by half, taste and add more if you wish. Also, keep in mind that the most potent heat in any hot pepper comes from capsaicin found in the seeds and the pith. To tone down the heat, remove these parts before using hot peppers, and consider wearing kitchen gloves when preparing them. Capsaicin can linger on your skin and cause a burning sensation.

When I worked in the test kitchen at *Chatelaine* magazine, I learned a great tip from one of my colleagues: Peel pieces of fresh ginger and store them in a freezer bag or a container in the freezer. Then next time you need some ginger, you can grate it from frozen.

Triple X Spicy Sambal

There are many ways to make sambal, a spicy Indonesian pepper condiment or relish found throughout Southeast Asia. Basic versions include hot peppers, garlic, ginger, and shrimp paste. Additional ingredients, such as nuts, vary, as every cook that makes this has their own version. Many years ago, after watching Ming Tsai make sambal on his cooking show, *East Meets West with Ming Tsai*, I was inspired to make my own to add to our burgers and anything else we wanted to boost with additional flavour.

MAKES ABOUT 1 CUP

10 raw or roasted unsalted cashews (optional)
4 jalapeño peppers, coarsely chopped (see Tip)
2 Thai red or green chili peppers, coarsely chopped (see Tip)
1 shallot, coarsely chopped
3 cloves garlic, coarsely chopped
2 Tbsp minced peeled fresh ginger (see Tip)
¼ cup avocado oil or sunflower oil
2 Tbsp fresh lime juice
2 tsp liquid honey

Place all ingredients in the bowl of a food processor fitted with the steel blade. Pulse until the mixture becomes a thick paste, scraping down the sides of the bowl as needed.

Transfer to an airtight container and store in the refrigerator for up to 2 weeks.

Slather It with Sauce

Go beyond mustard, relish, and tomato ketchup with special Flavour Fix sauces for your burgers.

Bacon and Sundried Tomato Mayonnaise	**75**
Beet Ketchup	**76**
Easy Burger Sauce	**78**
Curry Yogurt Sauce	**79**
Zesty Herb Mayonnaise	**80**

Bacon and Sundried Tomato Mayonnaise

Anytime you cook bacon for breakfast, I suggest you make a bit extra to stir up this decadently flavoured mayonnaise. It is excellent on burgers but also works well as a sandwich spread and as a flavourful mayo in deviled eggs.

MAKES ABOUT 1 CUP

1 cup mayonnaise (see Variation)
½ cup finely chopped cooked bacon
¼ cup sundried tomatoes, packed in oil,
drained and finely chopped
2 Tbsp finely sliced green onion (green and
white parts)
1 clove garlic, minced
½ tsp finely ground black pepper
¼ tsp sea salt

Combine all ingredients in a bowl. Store in an airtight container in the refrigerator for up to 2 weeks.

VARIATION

You can easily make a vegan version of this mayonnaise by using your favourite vegan mayo and swapping the cooked bacon with 2 Tbsp sweet smoked paprika.

Beet Ketchup

This book didn't feel complete without the addition of a recipe for ketchup. I didn't want to add a recipe for tomato ketchup because I am happy to buy that. I wanted something divinely different, like this delicious beet ketchup. Australians (my husband included) like adding sliced beets to their burgers, which inspired me to develop this recipe.

MAKES ABOUT 1½ CUPS

1 lb cooked red beets, coarsely chopped (see Tip)
1 cup apple cider vinegar
½ cup brown sugar, loosely packed
½ small onion (yellow or red), coarsely chopped
¼ cup finely chopped fresh dill (fronds and stems)
¼ cup finely chopped fresh parsley leaves
½ tsp ground cumin
½ tsp sea salt
½ tsp finely ground black pepper

We don't mind putting in the effort to peel and cook beets at home, so we often prepare enough to enjoy some with dinner and to make a batch of this ketchup. If you would rather not cook beets, then go ahead and use drained canned beets instead.

Add beets, vinegar, brown sugar, and onion to a medium saucepan, and stir to combine. Set over high heat and bring to a boil. Reduce heat and simmer for about 15 minutes, or until onions are soft.

Remove pan from heat and stir in dill, parsley, cumin, salt, and black pepper. Carefully transfer mixture to the bowl of a food processor fitted with the steel blade. Pulse until smooth. Allow to cool before transferring to a resealable container.

Keeps well, refrigerated, for up to 2 weeks

Easy Burger Sauce

We like to have a "secret sauce" we share with friends and family when the burgers come out. This one can be whipped up easily with ingredients in the pantry. Try this using my Beet Ketchup for something extra special.

MAKES ABOUT ¾ CUP

½ cup mayonnaise
¼ cup ketchup
2 Tbsp finely chopped cornichons or
gherkins (see Tip)
½ tsp garlic powder
½ tsp onion powder
½ tsp sweet paprika

Combine all ingredients in a bowl. Store in an airtight container in the refrigerator for up to 2 weeks.

TIP

Cornichons, as they are called in France, are similar to gherkins, which get their name from the Dutch word *gurken,* meaning small pickled cucumber. The difference between these and regular pickled cucumbers is their size and the flavour profile of the brining liquid used to preserve them. Flavours you'll find in pickle making include tarragon, dill, pepper, and garlic, and the tangy vinegar pickle brine can be made sweet or salty.

Curry Yogurt Sauce

I can't remember the first time I tried dipping my French fries into a curry sauce, but I remember that I couldn't get enough of that delicious goodness. My version includes the herbal freshness of cilantro and a hint of sweetness from apricot jam.

MAKES ABOUT 1 CUP

1 cup plain Greek yogurt (see Variation and page 56)
2 Tbsp finely chopped fresh cilantro leaves
1 Tbsp apricot jam (optional)
1 tsp fresh lemon juice
2 tsp curry powder
¼ tsp garlic powder
¼ tsp onion powder
¼ tsp ground cumin powder
¼ tsp ground coriander powder
¼ tsp sea salt
¼ tsp finely ground black pepper

Combine all ingredients in a bowl. Store in an airtight container in the refrigerator for up to 2 weeks.

Plain unsweetened coconut yogurt is a tasty vegan alternative that works well in this recipe.

Zesty Herb Mayonnaise

When I have an abundance of herbs available in the garden, or little bits left over in the fridge, I like to make a batch of mayonnaise. This is great in burgers, sandwiches, or even spread on fish before grilling. Please don't feel you have to follow my combination—use whatever herbs you have handy. Taste test as you create your own mix and note what you like the most so you can make it again any time.

MAKES ABOUT 1 CUP

1 cup mayonnaise
¼ cup finely sliced fresh basil leaves (see Variation)
¼ cup finely sliced fresh parsley leaves
2 Tbsp finely sliced fresh chives
2 Tbsp finely sliced fresh cilantro leaves
2 Tbsp finely grated lemon zest
2 Tbsp fresh lemon juice
½ tsp ground cumin

Combine all ingredients in a bowl. Transfer to an airtight container and store in the refrigerator for up to 2 weeks.

 VARIATION

When I want to make this and need a super quick alternative to preparing fresh herbs, I mix a few tablespoons of basil or cilantro pesto into the mayonnaise. It's not the same, but it does the trick. Here's an extra tip: store some pesto in a small container in the freezer for times like this.

Bundle Your Burger

Essentially a sandwich, burgers come together when a patty is topped with all sorts of goodness and nestled between a bun.

There are various ways to enjoy a delicious, juicy burger, with or without tucking it into a traditional bun. And if you'd rather go without a bun of any kind, you can always load up your patty with all the fixings and eat it just like that.

Wheat bun options can include: white wheat, whole wheat, brioche, pretzel, naan, pita, tortilla, potato blend, ciabatta bread, focaccia, English muffin, Kaiser rolls, and sliced bread, biscuits or scones.

A variety of wheat alternatives also exist, including gluten-free or low-carb:

- Fold your burger and all the fixings into leaves of lettuce, kale, collard, or Swiss chard.

- Grill up two portobello mushroom caps (see how to prepare on page 9) and use them as an alternative to a bun.

- Thickly slice and grill up some eggplant, sweet potato, cauliflower, or pineapple for something totally different and tasty.

make every bite the best

However you decide to bundle your burger, you are now fully equipped with my favourite recipes, kitchen tips and tricks for making the most flavourful burgers.

Enjoy all the different ways you can Flavour Fix and bundle your burger to make every bite the best. Bon appétit, my burger-loving friends!

Voula

Voula is a Cordon Bleu–certified chef, food expert and consultant, cookbook author, illustrator, and educator.

Her writing has appeared in print and digital formats in a variety of publications, including *Bon Appétit, Canadian Living, National Post, Zoomer, Fresh Juice, Reader's Digest Canada, Best Health, Food & Drink,* and *Chatelaine,* where she was a contributing editor and associate culinary expert in their test kitchen.

Voula was an in-house chef expert on CBC Television's award-winning show *Steven and Chris.* She showcased her fuss-free cooking concepts and launched the Flavour Fix brand to national and syndicated audiences.

Her first cookbook, *Eat at Home*, features more than 150 recipes. Voula has also published an illustrated recipe card collection (the first in the series is *Greek Spoon Sweets*). She is working on her third cookbook, *Flavour Fix Everything*, along with a Flavour Fix product line.

Voula was born in Toronto and lived there until 2020, when she and her family moved to the beautiful Peterborough and Kawartha Lakes District in Ontario.

To learn more, visit **www.voulahalliday.com/about**

List of Recipes

Made in the USA
Monee, IL
25 September 2023

43361007R00057